Celebrating the Family

A Critique of the BSR report
Something to Celebrate

Francis Bridger

Vicar of St Mark's, Woodthorpe and
Associate Lecturer in Philosophy, St John's College, Nottingham

GROVE BOOKS LIMITED
RIDLEY HALL RD CAMBRIDGE CB3 9HU

Contents

Acknowledgements

My heartfelt thanks to those who read the draft of this essay and whose comments have been invaluable: Christina Baxter, Greg Forster, John Goldingay, Colin Hart, Ian Paul and Alan Storkey.

The Cover Illustration is by Peter Ashton

First Impression October 1995
ISSN 0951-2659
ISBN 1 85174 302 2

1
Introduction

Who would have thought that a 200 page report by an obscure working party of the Church of England's General Synod would make the headlines in all the national newspapers and provoke comment from every side? (One might also wonder, by the way, what happened to the claims that the church is irrelevant in modern society). This was the state of affairs in June 1995 upon the publication of *Something to Celebrate* (hereafter abbreviated to *STC*). Such was the strength of feeling in some quarters of the Church that an attempt was made a month later at General Synod to prevent the report from ever reaching the floor for debate.

Why and how did this situation come about? In 1991-2 General Synod was worried about family breakdown and cohabitation. Two debates showed that members were disturbed by the rising trends in both. The Board of Social Responsibility, therefore, as the Synod's social ethics think tank, commissioned a study on family life and established a working party under the Bishop of Sherwood to carry it out. *Something to Celebrate* is the outcome.

Irrespective of whether the report ever forms the basis for official Anglican policy, it deserves careful consideration. The working party offers some shrewd social analysis along with a number of significant recommendations for both Church and nation. Misgivings about its theological flaws apart, it is a good example of the tradition in Anglican social ethics of attempting to inform theological and moral reflection by empirical study. Without such a method, moral reasoning becomes detached from social context and runs the risk of collapsing into idealism.

Initial Reactions

A brief glance at the immediate reactions to *Something to Celebrate* reveals the potency of family questions in contemporary Western societies. Initially the secular press fastened on the report's discussion of sex. The working party's recommendations on cohabitation—especially its view that the phrase 'living in sin' should be dropped—occasioned many a headline and not a little ribaldry. Only when more reflective pieces emerged on the inside pages did the wider issues relating to family life get an airing.

By far the most interesting twist related to the minority-report-that-never-was. It transpired that one member of the working party, Dr Alan Storkey, lecturer in sociology at Oak Hill theological college, resigned two months before publication because his minority contribution expressing disagreement on a number of points was rejected even though reports on occasions do contain sections expressing a minority view.

Reaction to *STC* has shown that the Church is still able to secure a widespread hearing when it comments on social issues provided that it is speaking about a topical subject and that it has something provocative to say. It has also confirmed that the secular press is largely unable to handle religious issues. Only the broadsheets assign specialist correspondents to cover them (not always with understanding) whilst the tabloids simply look for sensation. The result is superficial understanding combined with overwhelmingly negative images of the Church. It is therefore crucial that those who draft reports and (more importantly) those who write the press summary (which is all that many journalists read) ask themselves how their words will be interpreted in Fleet Street.

2

Overview

Structure

Something to Celebrate divides neatly into four parts. Part one offers an empirical description of family life in Britain as it is today and as it has been in the past. In doing so, it draws heavily upon historical and sociological research from which it advances a central conclusion: that the fundamental characteristic of families through the ages is that no one family form has been the norm in any sense. Likewise in contemporary society the sheer diversity of family forms contrasts with the 'cereal packet' image of the two-parent household with 2.4 children (p 6). This diversity, it argues, ought to be seen as a positive development which is here to stay and which should be respected and welcomed (pp 6-7).

Part two is interpretative. It suggests ways of understanding and evaluating changes in family patterns and 'reflecting on what families are' (p 9). It is here that theology is brought to bear on the empirical evidence adduced in part one. The aim, the report declares, is 'to develop a Christian perspective on families' (p 9). It is in this section also that theology turns into ethics as the authors attempt both to set out the vision and values they wish to proclaim and their practical implications.

Part three presents a number of recommendations for social policy and for the Church's involvement in supporting families. These are put forward as the logical outcomes of parts one and two. If part one is descriptive and part two reflective, then part three is prescriptive. It moves decisively into the area of political and social action and, following Faith in the City ten years before, *STC* offers recommendations both for the Church and for the nation.

Part four (which is very brief) summarizes previous chapters and ends with a clarion call to the Church and society 'to be loving and neighbourly in the increasingly complex world of contemporary family and household life' and to be 'a source of hope and community in a world of alienation and anonymity' (p 209).

What is clear from reading the report is that very considerable weight is put upon the historical and sociological evidence contained in part one. The theological and ethical discussion that follows in later parts is in many ways dependent upon this. It is not simply that empirical material provides a context for theological and ethical discussion. Rather, it determines the selection and type of theological and ethical arguments that are brought into play and is used as justification for the theological and ethical conclusions which emerge. In practice, this means that theology and ethics are subordinated to a particular (some would say ideological) interpretation of family life.

In all important respects, then, the method in this report is the message. In the chapters that follow, therefore, we shall concentrate on the interaction between the authors' empirical, theological and ethical reasoning rather than their specific policy recommendations.

The Method Assessed

In a paper published in the journal *Crucible* prior to the publication of *STC*, Stephen Barton (a member of the working party) offered a starting point for discussion. He argued for 'a hermeneutic of suspicion in order to try to discern whether "the family" is being used as a weapon to serve the interests of a broader (and sometimes hidden) agenda.'[1]

Barton's suggestion is surely correct. 'The family' has become a vehicle for all sorts of ideological purposes—as his reference to conservative, liberal, feminist and radical agendas indicated. However, whereas Barton saw the need for a hermeneutic of suspicion in essentially political and social terms, we must broaden his point to include history, theology and ethics, not least the handling of these by *STC* itself. His observation that 'it is important to be aware of the ways in which "the family" tends to become a moral and political symbol' is apposite.

In broad terms the method adopted by the working party is constructed of five components:

1. The 'Both-And' Principle.

An important aspect of the report is that it elevates ambiguity to the status of high principle. The authors are at pains to point out that they are concerned for diversity and respect, that truth is complex and difficult to discern, and that in a society where 'a large variety of views are seen to be equally valid,' Christianity cannot be exempt from the dilemmas this poses (pp 17-18). Consequently, they assert that while 'as Christians we believe we have important certainties to uphold...what is more difficult is to translate such general beliefs into specific statements about family life' (p 29).

---

1 Stephen Barton, 'Towards a Theology of the Family' in *Crucible* Jan-Mar 1993, p 4. On the problem of ideology in the discussion of family, see Peter & Brigitte Berger, *The War Over the Family*, (Harmondsworth: Penguin, 1983). Also J F Gubrium & J Holstein, *What is Family?*, (Mountain View: Mayfield, 1990), chapter 8.

In many respects this is uncontentious. After all, Christians in Western societies do operate in a climate of pluralism and relativism while complexity has
always been the very stuff of ethics, theological or otherwise. However, *STC* does
more than state the obvious fact that the task of moral theology is problematic or
that there is no simplistic way of deducing specific situational ethical require-
ments from general principles. The report disavows even the possibility of arriving at definite conclusions on important and crucial issues. Indeed, in its advocacy
of diversity and respect as a central methodological principle, the report ends up
by endorsing conclusions which are not merely in tension with one another but
are logically and theologically contradictory. The 'Both-And' Principle turns out
not to enable the authors to arrive at synthesis (as they perhaps hoped) but to
result in their propounding contradictory viewpoints simultaneously.

2. The Primacy of Human Experience.

In both theology and ethics, *STC* deliberately takes contemporary experience
rather than orthodox theology or tradition as its starting point and as its final
authority. Whether represented by the human sciences of sociology, anthropol-
ogy and history, or whether expressed in the anecdotal evidence supplied by sub-
missions presented to the working party, human experience is assigned priority
over theology in arriving at theological and ethical conclusions. It is not simply
that *STC* adopts an action-reflection approach to doing theology; it is that human
experience and the human sciences are allowed to condition the theological proc-
ess from start to finish. They determine the range of questions that can be asked
and sit in judgment upon the answers theology provides. And where theology or
ethics offers conclusions that challenge contemporary experience or mores, *STC*
opts repeatedly for the latter and then casts around for theological justification. In
reality, whatever the authors say about the importance of 'critical theological reflection,' they slip into moving from critical engagement between human experience and theology to the subordination of theology.[2]

The consequence of this move should not be underestimated: it shifts the methodological centre of gravity away from theology to the human sciences and human experience. Whether the working party realizes the enormity of this remains
unclear. Nonetheless, this is what the report does in the name of theological reflection and pastoral concern. Categories such as truth and right are replaced by
those of helpfulness and appropriateness.

Just how great a methodological step this represents can be seen by contrast-
ing the working party's approach with that of the Reformers. According to Calvin,
theological studies (which include what we would now call moral theology) must
begin with 'the knowledge of God and ourselves.'[3] The order of priority is crucial.

---

2   For models of engagement between theology and psychology as an example of human science,
    see Francis Bridger & David Atkinson, *Counselling in Context*, (London: HarperCollins, 1994),
    chapter 3.
3   John Calvin, *Institutes of the Christian Religion*, (Grand Rapids: AP&A edn, 1970), Chapter I
    section 1.

It is only as we understand more of the nature and ways of God that we are enabled to grasp more of the nature and purposes of human life. As Paul Mickey has pointed out, 'Calvin's theological reasoning asserts that the organizing centre for all theological discussion and authority finally is God; it is not human experience.'[4]

Yet what happens in *STC* is that the 'organizing centre' is effectively neither theology, nor Scripture, nor tradition but interpretations of human experience offered principally by the human sciences, laden as they are with the values and world-views of late twentieth-century humanism, itself informed by a cacophony of post-Enlightenment liberalism, Marxism, feminism or whatever.

This is where Barton's warning becomes crucial. For if we apply a hermeneutic of suspicion to the theological and ethical method of *STC* we see that it is much more radical than the unsuspecting reader might suppose, that it is built upon a number of non-theological assumptions and thought-forms cloaked in theological language, and that it is ideologically driven.

3. Pluralism and Relativism.

In a highly significant discussion of the contemporary intellectual scene in the West, the working party notes that 'all disciplines, whether in the social or physical sciences, are now characterized by much greater uncertainty than in the past' (p 17). As a descriptive statement, this presents little with which to quibble. However, in a telling passage, the report goes on to offer what emerges as its own *credo*: 'Contradictory viewpoints may be held to be equally valid when examined within this more complex understanding of how truth is reached' (p 17).[5]

In voicing this, and in its subsequent discussions, the working party moves from description to prescription: it slips from describing the problem of arriving at conclusive statements to prescribing that this is how it should be. In answer to the question 'Does Christianity possess absolute and ultimate truth, so that it can stand in judgment upon other beliefs and provide clear moral guidelines?' it is unable to give a decisive answer, even in principle. The best it can say is that 'the debate between absolutes and possibles is a tension which runs through this report' (p 18).

In fact, the problem it describes is not one of tension between absolutes and possibles. To put it thus is quite misleading. If this were the essence of the debate, the working party would be able to offer a much more robust answer to its question. For the dilemma of how to act upon moral absolutes in a flawed world is one which has characterized Jewish and Christian moral theology from the beginning. Rather the question is whether even in principle Christianity should be regarded as capable of making theological and moral claims which are authoritative over and against other claims. About this *STC* remains equivocal.

This throws up a problem which the working party never adequately addresses,

---

4   Paul A. Mickey, *Of Sacred Worth*, (Nashville: Abingdon Press, 1991) p 77.
5   On this see, for example, David Lyon, *Postmodernity*, (Buckingham: OUP, 1994).

namely, that its methodological assumptions prevent it from offering any substantial critique of pluralism and relativism just at those points where such a critique is needed.[6] The best it can do is to make statements which might seem anodyne such as 'We offer challenging ways forward for families but we do not give easy answers' (p 7) and 'The Christian vision is a vision of the truth. It is…about discovering reality and becoming more real in the way we live' (p 8). Consequently, the problems posed by pluralism and relativism are never really faced. This, in turn, makes it extraordinarily difficult for *STC* to generate any coherent organizing concepts for its theology of the family or for its ethical discussion other than the single, unexplained appeal to love (left undefined and unexamined).[7] As we shall see, this amounts to a fundamental weakness which runs right through the report's reasoning at every level.

4. Sociology

It is difficult for a non-sociologist to offer a criticism of sociological method. However, one point is relevant: the working party sent out 25,000 questionnaires to individuals and organisations in order to ascertain views on the state of family life today. This method is extolled and commended as an example for other working parties to follow (p 5). But one does not have to be a sociologist to ask a number of questions. On what basis were recipients selected? By what criteria were the questions devised? Why did the working party opt for open-ended rather than closed questions? What professional advice was sought and acted upon in the construction of the questionnaire? Why was no social scientific analysis made of the results?

These questions are important because the working party places so much emphasis upon the findings from the questionnaire. They are also pertinent because only 1000 replies were received—a fact which is revealed only in an appendix (in contrast to the trumpeting in the introductory chapter of the fact that 25,000 were sent out) and which must cast serious doubt upon the conclusions the working party draws. In professional survey terms, a response rate of only 4% is very small indeed and certainly cannot be reckoned to provide authoritative data for the kind of categorical claims *STC* makes.

Moreover, by the very nature of the questions—open ended, subjective and imprecise—the responses were bound to be highly anecdotal. They require very careful interpretation indeed, for there is no way of checking either the truthfulness of respondents or the accuracy of their answers.[8] In matters which by definition are highly personal, and in many cases the occasion of considerable pain, the

---

6 For a critique of relativism, see Roger Trigg, *Reason and Commitment*, (Cambridge: CUP, 1973).

7 This, of course, was the programme offered by situation ethics.

8 See Michael Drake & Ruth Finnegan (eds), *Sources and Methods for Family and Community Historians: A Handbook*, (Cambridge: Open University/CUP, 1994). Speaking of questionnaires, they comment that 'they have the disadvantage that, however carefully questions are formulated and pre-tested, some misunderstandings are almost unavoidable, and personal variations are squeezed into preset categories to give a possibly spurious impression of objectivity.'

responses can offer only partial and highly subjective interpretations of experiences to which the questioner has no independent access.

5. Moral Theology.

STC is concerned to uphold and preserve families as places where human good is promoted and human flourishing encouraged. The problem arises when the report tries to move from general statements about values and goals to discerning what goodness and flourishing actually consist in. It is clear that qualities such as love, peace, joy and other fruits of the Spirit are to be reckoned as good. What *STC* lacks is any coherent account of the relationship between these and moral theology as a whole.

Morality in this sense should not be taken primarily to mean a set of commands or rules. Such a view of Christian ethics is at best incomplete. Rather, it has to do with the theological framework out of which principles, paradigms and commands are developed. For morality is a deliberative exercise. It is not a matter of 'reading off' instructions from the Bible or a theological text, nor is it a matter of jumping straight into the moral situation. The ethical task involves deliberation and reflection both upon the sources of theological reasoning and upon the empirical reality to which this must be applied.[9]

The central problem in *STC*, however, is that while it presents the reader with a considerable number of ethical conclusions, it shows little sign of grounding such conclusions in a coherent moral theological method. Nor does it offer ways of moving from values and principles to concrete situations.

This is not the same as saying that the report lacks theological discussion. Chapter 5, 'Theological Perspectives on Families' is an explicit attempt to relate theology to human life and experience. The problem is that it draws very little on moral or systematic theology. Instead, it offers a series of insights under the headings of 'Help from the Bible' and 'Help from the Church's Tradition' and then seeks to draw out 'practical implications.' The result is a collection of 'perspectives' in the following order: 'The Christian Understanding of God'; 'Mature Personhood'; 'Marriage'; 'Children'; 'Diverse Family Forms'; 'Church and Family'; 'Sin'; 'Salvation.' Merely to read this list indicates the need for a method to demonstrate the relationship between the parts and the whole. In short, what the report requires is moral theology in addition to ethical comment.

---

9   Oliver O'Donovan, 'Christian Moral Reasoning' in David Atkinson & David Field (eds), *New Dictionary of Christian Ethics and Pastoral Theology*, (Leicester: IVP, 1995) pp 122-27. Thomas Ogletree, *The Use of the Bible in Christian Ethics*, (Philadelphia: Fortress, 1983).

3

History

In *Something to Celebrate* history is central to the authors' case. It is used to suggest that family forms are relative to cultures and periods in history, and that no trans-historical or trans-cultural claims can be made for the normativity (in any sense) of the conjugal nuclear family. This historical point is then invoked to reinforce the theological view that diversity and variety of family forms are part of God's purpose and that no one form can be regarded as paradigmatic. Consequently, if history, theology and ethics are thus intertwined, it follows that the report's reasoning in all three must be critically scrutinized. It also follows that if *STC*'s historical claims are called into question, support for its theological and ethical assertions is thereby weakened. It is this nexus we shall be considering in the present and following chapters.

Historical Method

All disciplines involve selection and interpretation of data, and history is no exception. However, critical historical method requires three things: (a) that the historian be able to articulate the criteria by which she chooses some data and not others; (b) that she be aware of her own biases and predilections in adducing and interpreting evidence; and (c) that she demonstrate that she has tested the evidence by pitting it against alternative data and interpretations. Without these, history collapses into ideology.[10] Unfortunately, *STC* does exactly this as two examples will illustrate.

1. The Golden Age

The authors of the report are insistent that there has never been 'a golden age' of family life. They note, however, that many people who wrote to the working party clearly thought there had been and that we have fallen away from it. Such correspondents, according to the report, 'looked back with yearning to what they thought had been a golden age of moral certainty and family stability' (p 18). This perception, it argues, has 'more to do with powerful hidden persuaders which present quite unrealistic, sentimentalized images of the family, suitable only for marketing washing powder or breakfast cereals with no bearing on reality' (p 74). This reality is that 'although the family is a God-given context for human nurture and blessing, it may also be life-destroying' (p 75).

The notion of a golden age, therefore, should be seen entirely as a wishful projection back into history by troubled twentieth century societies, 'a metaphor for how people wished their lives had been.' Consequently, 'the idea of the family

---

10 On historical method and philosophy see Colin Brown (ed), *History, Criticism and Faith*, (Leicester: IVP, 1976) pt III.

has a powerful grip on people's imaginations and represents something over and above their actual experience.' Why this imaginary 'golden age' should have been constructed in the first place has to do with the pace of change in modern societies and the need to hang onto a symbol which offers reassurance and continuity. The family, therefore, expresses 'perhaps more vividly than any other idea a sense of collective well-being' (p 18).

There is a certain plausibility about this, especially when family life is perceived by many to be under threat. However, a number of points are relevant here. Firstly, it is not quite clear who actually is claiming that a golden age (in the sense defined by the working party) ever existed. The report does not cite sources for the claim other than those who wrote in. Consequently, the depiction presented in the report looks suspiciously like an Aunt Sally—easy to erect and easy to knock down.

Secondly, certain specific historical statements in *STC* are highly questionable. One example is the report's assertion that:

> 'At the beginning of the nineteenth century, about 60 per cent of first births in England were conceived outside marriage, a figure which suggests levels of premarital sexual activity not markedly lower than at the present day.' (p 22).

This claim is difficult to assess since the source for it is not cited. Yet such a general and categorical assertion requires to be substantiated. Is the claim based on evidence which can be taken to apply to the country as a whole? Or is it based on local sources? Indeed, what kind of evidence could yield the startling conclusions that the working party advances?[11]

The difficulty is compounded by evidence that is in the public domain, regarding illegitimacy. Here there are good grounds for questioning *STC*'s interpretation of sexual activity. Prior to 1840, births were registered with ecclesiastical authorities. After this date they began to be registered by the state. Comparison of the two reveals that between 1800 and 1840, illegitimacy rose from only 5% to 6%.[12]

Premarital conceptions are not the same as illegitimate births, of course. But when we consider that today's illegitimacy rate is 31% (p 306) the report's claim that premarital sexual activity has not varied much over the past 200 years is difficult to believe. It is likely, of course, that in the nineteenth century a number of premarital conceptions would have turned into legitimate births as couples got married once they discovered the woman was pregnant. But if the report is to be believed, that figure would have to have been phenomenal—from 60% to 6% in fact. This is simply not credible.

Thirdly, *STC*'s contention that marriage based on love is a recent invention

---

11 This is but one example of a repeated tendency of *STC* to make large, categorical general claims unsupported by evidence either in the text or in footnotes.
12 Peter Laslett, *Family Life and Illicit Love in Earlier Generations*, (Cambridge: CUP, 1977) chapter 3, especially pp 104 & 113.

must be regarded as one-sided at best. According to the working party, in pre-industrial times

'Amongst even the smallest landowners, marriage remained essentially a property deal and marriages were arranged by the spouses' parents. Though love did flourish in many marriages, romantic love existed primarily in the courtly tradition when it was associated with a chaste commitment outside the marriage bond.' (p 21).

The chairman, moreover, was keen to make the same point to the wider public through the columns of a national newspaper. Writing in the *Daily Mirror*, he insisted that:

'We should not be looking back at the golden age of family. In fact, marriage for love is a fairly new idea. People used to get married for much more practical reasons, such as keeping land and property within the family.' (7th June 1995)

This is, however, only one possible interpretation. Historically, there is good evidence to suggest the very opposite from what the report claims. Firstly, scholarship over the last 25 years has called into question whether courtly love in the form mentioned by *STC* even existed. One historian has gone so far as to argue that it is a myth.[13]

Secondly, that some people did marry for land and property cannot be disputed. But how widespread this was is another question. It was by definition confined to those who possessed such things, namely the upper classes. The majority of people married for other reasons, including affection and love.

One clue to understanding this lies in the ages at which people married. The earlier their ages, the greater the likelihood of an arranged marriage for material reasons and not a marriage based on mutual consent. Here, as we have seen, the report is insistent that even among the lower classes this was the norm.

There is evidence, however, that most marriages were contracted relatively late in people's lives (bearing in mind their life expectancy), which suggests that they married for reasons other than property, land or wealth. Thus according to Lawrence Stone, between the sixteenth and the eighteenth centuries the median age of first marriage among small property owners and labourers rose from 27 to 28 for men and from 24 to 27 for women.[14] In Stone's words, 'It has now been established beyond any doubt that all over north-west Europe…the middle and lower classes of both sexes married remarkably late, certainly from the fifteenth

---

13 On the existence or otherwise of courtly love, see D N Robertson (ed), *The Meaning of Courtly Love*, (New York, 1968) p 1.

14 Lawrence Stone, *The Family, Sex and Marriage in England 1500-1800*, (London: Weidenfeld & Nicholson, 1977) p 50.

century onwards.'[15]

The significance of such evidence is that it flatly contradicts one plank of the historical platform on which the authors of *STC* build their case. If this component of the golden age actually did exist—contrary to the working party's contention—it means that we must be wary of other historical claims also.

Literary sources offer further evidence. Whereas statistical evidence supplies us with what people did, literary evidence enables us to see what they felt. Here as early as the fourteenth century we are presented with a picture of popular belief that marriage should be for love rather than gain. For example William Langland, the author of Piers Plowman, wrote in the 1370s that true marriage was 'for love and not for property.'[16] A century later, *The Boke of Good Manners* (a best-seller translated from French by Caxton in 1487) affirmed emphatically that marriage is ordained 'for to love each other' and goes on to decry marriages that are made 'for money or other evil cause.'[17] Seven years later in 1494 Sebastian Brant wrote in another European best-seller *The Ship of Fools* that:

Who weds and for naught else is fain
Than growth of property and gain
Will suffer quarrels, woe and pain.[18]

And so the evidence continues. Henry VIII's Lord Deputy at Calais, Arthur Lisle, corresponded with his wife while they were separated for two brief periods in the 1530s. The letters have survived and reveal an intense love between the two, employing such terms as 'Sweete hart' and 'Mine own sweete hart.'[19] Meanwhile, Lisle's scribe in Calais could write to his wife as 'mine own sweet heart and entirely beloved bedfellow in as much as heart can desire.'[20] These sentiments, we need to remember, were penned by bureaucrats schooled in the art of not betraying personal feelings on paper. That they should have done so suggests that, despite the complexity of the issue, romantic love has a much longer history than *STC* will allow.

The same thoughts can be found, moreover, in documents surviving from the seventeenth century. Ralph Josselin, an Essex clergyman and small farmer's son, tells us that he fell in love when he first saw his wife in 1639. His diary records that 'my eye fixed with love upon a maid, and hers upon me, who afterwards

---

15 See also the massive contribution of Peter Laslett and the Cambridge Group for the History of Population and Social Structure in such works as Peter Laslett, *The World We Have Lost*, (London 1965); Peter Laslett & Richard Wall, *Household and Family in Past Time*, (Cambridge: CUP, 1972); Peter Laslett, *Family Life and Illicit Love in Earlier Generations*, (Cambridge: CUP, 1977); Richard Wall, Peter Laslett & Jean Robin, *Family Forms in Historic Europe*, (Cambridge: CUP, 1983).

16 quoted in Ferdinand Mount, *The Subversive Family*, (London: Unwin, 1982) p 70.

17 quoted in Mount, *ibid* p 69.

18 Sebastian Brant, *The Ship of Fools*, trans Edwin Zeydel (New York: Dover Publications, 1962 edn) p 182.

19 Muriel St Clair Byrne, *The Lisle Letters, Vol 1*, (Chicago: Chicago University Press, 1981) p 5.

20 *Ibid*, p 353.

proved my wife.'[21] Similarly, Oliver Heywood, a nonconformist minister and son of a Lancashire yeoman wrote after his wife's death in 1642 that 'She was as loving a wife as ever lay in any man's bosome, if she offended in any way it was through vehemency of affection, the lord brought us together and continued our relation in abundance of mercy, for which I haue cause to blesse him whiles I lieue.'[22]

What we have, then, is a picture quite at odds with the claims made by *STC*. Far from being a modern phenomenon, marriage based on romantic love predated the Romantic revolution of the eighteenth century. It was not a question, for most people, of marriage being contracted for property, money or land. Love and affection proved far more common motives. And even when material gain was relevant, it was the case among only a small proportion of the population. For the majority, love and marriage went together.

We have seen how the report's claims about a supposed golden age are one-sided. We must now turn to the central claim of the historical relativist thesis, namely that the conjugal nuclear family is a peculiarly modern phenomenon.

2. The Conjugal Nuclear Family[23]

STC expresses considerable doubts about the nuclear family both historically and theologically. We shall examine the theological arguments in chapter 4. But for the moment we need to test its claim that the conjugal nuclear family is suspect because it is a peculiarly modern invention.

The point of such a claim is to reject the nuclear family as in any sense normative. By insisting on its historical and cultural relativity, the working party attempts to bolster the theological assertion that 'no single form of the family is a kind of God-given ideal' (p 87). Indeed, since 'one dimension of God's goodness is clearly to be seen in the rich diversity of creation and the ways in which human beings live together in their different cultures and societies,' it follows that 'the findings of historians of the family help us to appreciate the diversity…' (p 87). The historical relativity of the nuclear family is thus crucial to *STC*'s case.

When we look at the historical evidence, however, it becomes clear that the conjugal nuclear family cannot be written off so easily. Far from being the 'primarily modern, urban development' (p 75) the report supposes, it has a much longer history than the authors are prepared to acknowledge.

Once again, the working party seems not to have taken seriously the body of evidence developed by historians from the mid nineteen-sixties onwards. The cumulative result of such research is that, in the words of sociologists Peter and Brigitte Berger, 'the notion that the nuclear family is an exclusive product of mo-

---

21 See Alan MacFarlane (ed), *The Diary of Ralph Josselin*, (Cambridge: CUP, 1976); *The Family Life of Ralph Josselin*, (Cambridge: CUP, 1970) pp 106-7.
22 quoted in Mount, *op cit*, pp 88-9.
23 For the use of conjugality as a defining criterion of family, see Peter Laslett, *Household and Family in Past Time, op cit*, pp 28ff.

dernity can itself be shown to have been a myth.'[24]

What is this evidence which undermines *STC*'s historical relativism? First, research has shown that as far back as Anglo-Saxon times marriage was monogamous and society was marked by the primacy of the nuclear family.[25] Second, the persistence of the nuclear family in western Europe stretched through the middle ages into the pre-modern period and beyond. A study of the fourteenth century French village of Montaillou, for example, revealed that families bore a striking resemblance to the kind of nuclear family *STC* reckons to have been the product of the Industrial Revolution four centuries later.[26] Moreover, when household sizes are studied, it emerges that they remained remarkably stable throughout the period from 1574 to 1901 at a mean of 4.75 persons. As Peter Laslett has commented:

'In England and elsewhere in Northern and Western Europe the standard situation was one where each domestic group consisted of a simple family living in its own house, so that the conjugal family was identical with the household.'[27]

Laslett's study also explodes the myth of the preindustrial extended family, a myth explicitly endorsed by *STC* in its attempt to show the modernity of the nuclear family. According to the report,

'In the relatively closed and stable rural communities, the extended family network continued to play an important role, a role which survived greater urbanisation to a marked extent.' (p 21)

What the work of Laslett and others has demonstrated is that exactly the opposite is the case. In England during the period 1574-1821, not only were household sizes stable, as we have seen, but the number of households containing more than three generations was tiny at only 5.8% of the total.[28] This pattern was repeated throughout northern Europe and colonial North America. As Laslett notes:

'There is no sign of the large, extended co-residential group of the traditional peasant world giving way to the small, nuclear, conjugal household of modern industrial society.'[29]

24 Brigitte & Peter Berger, *op cit*, p 98.
25 Lorraine Lancaster, 'Kinship in Anglo-Saxon Society' in *The British Journal of Sociology Vol 9* (1958) pp 230-50, 359-77.
26 Brigitte & Peter Berger, *ibid*, p 99.
27 The findings of Laslett and others are surveyed in J E Goldthorpe, *Family Life in Western Societies*, (Cambridge: CUP, 1987) pp 19ff. For a survey of approaches to family history in general, see Michael Anderson, *Approaches to the History of the Western Family 1500-1914*, (London: Macmillan, 1980).
28 *Ibid*, p 21.
29 *Ibid*, p 19.

In the words of J E Goldthorpe, writing in 1987, 'the large, joint or extended family seemed never to have existed at any time covered by the records.'[30]

In fact, it now seems that the extended family was much more a product of industrialisation than was once recognized or than the working party even acknowledges. It used to be thought that the rise of the factory system caused the splitting up of rural families as family members migrated to the towns in search of work. What appears to have happened, however, is that once families established themselves in towns, they brought their wider kin to join them. To quote Goldthorpe once more:

'It seems, then, that the rise of industry led to family members living together in close proximity, and created bigger family groups and greater cohesion than in pre-industrial times, not the other way round.'[31]

What are we to make, then, of STC's use of history? And what significance does it hold?

Perhaps the most apparent thing is the extreme selectivity which governs the working party's handling of historical evidence. It is true that it tries to hedge its bets slightly on the nuclear family by speaking of its roots going back to the fourteenth century (p21). But the overwhelming force of STC's argument is that, whatever such qualifying phrases might mean, the authors believe the nuclear family to be essentially modern.

This selectivity distorts both the report's historical method and its conclusions. At every important point of debate it opts for one-sided evidence only. What is more, it produces little direct evidence in support of its statements, either in the text or in footnotes. And where evidence is cited, it is invariably used to support sweeping categorical conclusions of the kind we have observed. Alternative interpretations are ignored or dismissed with the result that there is no real sense of historical debate.

Secondly, it is striking that the working party has opted in every case for historical interpretations which are now widely recognized as out-dated. There has been enough work produced by professional historians since the mid-1960s to overturn previous interpretations of the family without opting for revisionism for its own sake. Yet the report seems not to know this; or if it does, it does not admit so. It is hard to escape the conclusion that the report is not seriously interested in critical historical method but only in using history to support conclusions arrived at on other grounds. To what these might be we must now turn.

---

30 *Loc cit.*
31 *Ibid,* p 33.

4
Theology

The criticisms of *STC*'s method outlined in previous chapters come to a head in the report's discussion of family forms, alternative families and human sexuality. In this chapter we shall see how the lack of a clearly articulated moral theology results in conclusions which amount to little more than legitimations of contemporary social liberalism.

Family Forms
As we have seen, *STC* emphatically rejects the view that the conjugal nuclear family should be regarded in any way as historically or theologically paradigmatic. The theological argument can be summarized thus: families exist so that God's love may be shared and human beings enabled to flourish. This does not require any particular form of family life. Divine love and human flourishing can be mediated by a variety of family structures, none of which should be assigned priority. To assume that the conjugal nuclear family represents a God-given ideal is close to idolatry. Moreover, neither history nor theology support the view that such families are anything more than culture-relative. To see the nuclear family as more than this is to make 'Christian truth about people-in-relationship…captive to "tribal" interests of one kind or another' (p 87).

A number of things are significant about this line of reasoning. Firstly, there is the language. What does it mean to speak of 'making truth captive to tribal interests?' This appears to be nothing more than language used emotively to disparage views other than those held by the working party.

Secondly, we need to note that according to *STC* family should be defined by the quality of relationships within domestic groups rather than by any particular form such groups might take. It does not matter whether families comprise nuclear, lone-parent or lesbian and gay relationships; the crucial point is that they manifest qualities such as love, peace and joy which enable human flourishing to take place.[32]

Thirdly, such a view undercuts an orthodox doctrine of creation. The traditional interpretation of Genesis 1 and 2 emphasizes the givenness of the conjugal, heterosexual family as part of the created order which is trans-cultural and trans-historical. In other words, the symbolism of the Adam-Eve pairing is that they

---

32 As argued by a member of the working party, Sue Waldrond-Skinner, in her book *The Fulcrum and the Fire*, (London: Darton, Longman & Todd, 1993). See especially her discussion of the 'deconstruction and reconstruction of marriage and the family' (pp 25ff) and her claim that 'since the Lord is eternally creating all things new, we should expect to be continually surprised by the new forms and structures into which God is calling human beings to bear witness to his life and love.'(p 47) This betrays a serious confusion about the concept of created order and its relationship to morality. See Oliver O'Donovan, *Resurrection and Moral Order*, (Leicester/Grand Rapids: IVP/Eerdmans, 1986) part one.

offer a universal paradigm for the essence of what it means to be a family. The working party never really comes to grips with this interpretation. Its discussion of the creation narratives all but sidesteps the question of family form. In offering an exposition of their meaning, it significantly chooses only to draw from 'the beautiful and intimate story of the man and woman' a truth about relationships: 'that the way individual people find their true identity is through their relations with God, with fellow human beings, with themselves and with the rest of creation' (p 76).

As far as it goes this cannot be denied. But as an interpretation of Genesis 1 and 2, it is too partial. The fact that there has existed a long tradition which assigns to these chapters a paradigmatic significance cries out for much more theological discussion than the report supplies. If there is to be a true quest for the passages' meaning, to interpret them primarily in relational terms simply will not do.

Is there anything else that can be said to be trans-cultural and trans-historical? Do the creation narratives offer us anything more that can be reckoned as universally paradigmatic? The working party surprisingly insists they do: values and qualities such as those associated in the New Testament with the fruit of the Spirit. These, rather than a particular family form, are the true trans-cultural and trans-historical truths.

It is a neat argument. But although it offers a way out of the problem of hermeneutical distance, it does so at considerable cost. For once it is accepted that family forms are irrelevant provided that they embody the kind of relational qualities deemed to be good, the givenness of creation itself becomes questionable. We are forced to ask whether there is any connection, theological or otherwise, between values and qualities on one hand and their embodiment in particular structures and forms of life on the other. According to the working party's reasoning, there is not. As long as the values themselves are expressed relationally, it does not matter what form these relationships adopt.

The logical effect of this must be to create a kind of dualistic split in which the physical is downgraded in favour of the spiritual, a step which no doubt would be abhorrent to the working party. The traditional view of creation was designed to prevent such dualism by insisting that form and value were aspects of a single unity. Hence the belief that the creation narratives do more than tell us about the importance of relational qualities. They remind us that God purposely embodied these in specific forms of life. Consequently the moral order is rooted and reflected in the created order. The structures of creation must not be regarded as value-neutral but as mediators of the moral order established by God himself. All this is lost once values are sheared off from forms in the way *STC* suggests.

It follows from all this that we must view the conjugal heterosexual family far more paradigmatically than the working party accepts. For if form and value are of a piece, the creation narratives do offer us a paradigm. Moreover, Scripture as a whole takes as normative the conjugal family unit. Despite the various patterns of family portrayed in both Old and New Testaments, they share one thing in

18

common: that the conjugal family is fundamental and cannot be discarded merely as an act of human will. Whether the kinship networks of Israel or the households of the gospels and epistles, all assumed that God had created the mother-father-children relationship as universal and trans-historical.[33]

Alternative Families

If conjugal nuclear families are not the norm but merely one 'prototype' among many, what are the alternatives? Here *STC* is insistent that not anything goes. There are some limits as to what count as acceptable family forms. However, on the kind of reasoning we have already noted, it is hard to see exactly what these might be. Hence we are brought to the two most controversial parts of the report: its discussion of cohabitation and gay and lesbian families.

1. Cohabitation

The working party is realistic about cohabitation in contemporary society. It notes that the majority of couples who get married have previously cohabited and offers a shrewd analysis of why this might be so. All this is to be welcomed as confirmation of the trend that parish clergy have been aware of for some time. It is when the report moves from describing the current situation to an ethical evaluation that problems arise.

Principal among these is the working party's explicit avowal of a 'Both-And' approach. It wants to affirm the validity of both marriage and cohabitation. Thus on one hand it proclaims that 'the Christian practice of lifelong, monogamous marriage lies at the heart of the Church's understanding of how the love of God is made manifest in the sexual companionship of a man and a woman' (p 118). Yet on the other, it believes that 'some forms of cohabitation are marriages already in all but name' (p 116) and should be treated as if they were marriages. It is this attempt to embrace contradictory viewpoints simultaneously that many have found difficult to accept.

But why should this be so? Does not common sense endorse the working party's approach? Perhaps, but at a high price. For in the end, we are left with three choices in terms of ethics:

1. Marriage and cohabitation are equally valid;
2. Marriage and cohabitation are not equally valid but can, in principle, both be good;
3. Marriage and cohabitation are mutually exclusive.

3 For a discussion of Israelite family forms and how to derive contemporary norms and family structures from them see Michael Schluter and Roy Clements, *Reactivating the Extended Family*, (Cambridge: Jubilee Centre, 1986). Also, C J H Wright, *Living as the People of God*, (Leicester: IVP, 1983) and C J H Wright, *God's People in God's Land: Family, Land and Property in the Old Testament* (Grand Rapids: Eerdman's, 1990). For a more general discussion of the theology of family, see Michael Moynagh, 'Home to Home: Towards a Biblical Model of the Family' in *Anvil* 3:3 (1986) pp 209-29. Also David Atkinson, *Pastoral Ethics in Practice*, (Eastbourne: Monarch, 1989) chapter 6.

The traditional Christian view would affirm option 3. *STC* rejects this because to rule out cohabitation absolutely would be to reject the possibility that some couples might choose to live together for morally valid reasons. It would also amount to a denial of current social trends which need to viewed 'with sympathy and discernment' (p 118). Moreover, a rejectionist stance would alienate the very generation of young people the Church is desperate to reach.

But neither does the working party opt for 1. True to its relational criteria, it recognizes that some partnerships may be far from loving, caring and supportive. Cohabitation is no guarantee of successful relationships and, moreover, it may be undertaken for the wrong reasons. Where this is the case, cohabitation should not be regarded as morally defensible (but then neither should marriage).

However, some cohabitations are to all intents and purposes marriages without the benefit of ceremony, and it is these which the report identifies as morally good. Pointing out that the public ceremony of marriage merely confirms the consent and commitment two people make to each other, rather than creating them, the working party goes on to argue that 'in terms of the theology of marriage, cohabitation which involves a mutual, lifelong, exclusive commitment may be a legitimate form of marriage...' (p 116). Where such relationships exist, it is possible to see that 'the fruits of love, joy, peace, patience, gentleness and self-control can be harvested within cohabiting relationships as they can be in marriage' (p 113).

At this point it becomes clear that the working party opts for a combination of 1 and 2. In doing so it tries to be sensitive to all sides of the debate. By contrast, would argue for a modified version of 3 which sought to uphold the primacy of marriage while recognizing that if couples cohabit it is better that they do so committed to each other in stable, long-term relationships than in other forms of cohabitation. *STC*'s views, however, need to be challenged on a number of grounds.

Firstly, although *STC* acknowledges that cohabitation can be risky and fragile and is often undertaken for wrong reasons, it nonetheless gives a more optimistic impression of cohabitation than the evidence warrants. We have only to look at the report's empirical section to appreciate this. According to the working party

'The period of cohabitation tends to be short-lived. One-third of couples cohabit for less than a year and only 16 per cent live with their partner for more than five years. A cohabiting relationship lasts two years on average and then the couple either separate or marry.' (p 34).

Moreover, it appears that couples who marry having first cohabited are '50 per cent more likely to have divorced within five years of marrying than those who did not previously cohabit' (p 114). This picture is confirmed by a report from the Joseph Rowntree Foundation which states that cohabitees are four times more likely to separate than married couples. It is hard to see, therefore, why the working party is so ready to accept cohabitation as a trend to be accommodated. From society's point of view, let alone that of the Church or individual couples, cohab tation is decidedly more unstable than marriage and therefore to be discouraged.

Secondly, the report's 'Both-And' approach ends up satisfying nobody. Committed cohabitees of the kind the report accepts as married in all but name might reasonably ask what value there would be in marrying. If the fruits of the Spirit can be experienced without the formality of marriage, why bother? Conversely, for the couple wondering whether to get married, the knowledge that cohabitation is morally valid provides no incentive for marriage. The working party's contention that cohabitation 'is an opportunity and challenge to the Church to articulate its doctrine of marriage in ways so compelling…that the institution of marriage regains its centrality' (p 118) is simply naive.

Thirdly, at the theological level it is unclear exactly what the report believes marriage is. It does not offer either one model or a synthesis of models. It does offer a series of 'perspectives' but these are simply laid alongside one another without any serious attempt to relate them or to develop a coherent theology of either marriage or family. The nearest it comes to doing so is a brief acknowledgment that a covenantal model has something to teach us (p 86). But this reference is very brief indeed and the notion is left unexplored.

Yet it is at this point that the working party presented itself and its readers with a golden opportunity. The 'big theological idea' (for example, that of covenant) which is so lacking throughout the report could have been developed in depth. Moreover, the concept of covenant offers itself for this purpose precisely because there exists a history of covenant theology which is both rich and deep. This theology has been employed to articulate all kinds of social relationship from the citizen's relation to the state, to marriage and family. It offers a starting point for exactly the discussion and theological exploration the report says is needed.[34]

Fourthly, if some kinds of cohabitation and marriage are to be regarded as equivalent, what are we to make of the significance of a public ceremony? *STC* is ambiguous about this. It concedes the importance of the ceremony but fails to follow its reasoning through. Indeed, its discussion moves on rapidly from acknowledging that 'theologically and morally what makes a marriage is the freely given consent and commitment in public of both partners' (p 116) to setting out reasons why cohabitation is an acceptable alternative. The result is that the more we examine what the report actually says, the more difficult it becomes to reconcile what, in effect, are contradictory positions.[35]

Fifthly, many will find unacceptable the explicit association of the list of fruits of the Spirit with pre- or quasi-marital relationships. For these are fruits of holiness and of the activity of the Spirit of God, not merely virtuous human qualities. They

---

34 See Francis Bridger, *Theology and Politics in the English Revolution 1640-1660*, (unpub PhD thesis, Bristol, 1980) chapter 2. For a modern covenant theology of family, see Ray S Anderson & Dennis B Guernsey, *On Being Family*, (Grand Rapids: Eerdmans, 1985) chapter 2.

35 *STC*'s position seems to be that marriages without the benefit of ceremony (so-called common-law marriages) should be regarded as equal in status to legal marriages. If so, it is seriously remiss in failing to suggest in its Recommendations to the Nation (pp 213ff) that co-habitants be extended the formal legal protection given by marriage in the event of intestate death, arguments over joint property etc.

must therefore be embedded in structures which reflect holiness.

Finally, to argue for the conjugal nuclear family as paradigmatic is not to say that other quasi-conjugal forms are incapable of deep and loving relationships. To do so would fly in the face of experience. But here we come to a fundamental theological point: such forms may approximate to the paradigm to a greater or lesser degree but this does not make them equivalent to it. Moreover, to rule out the possibility of a paradigm on the ground that some may not fit it and will therefore feel judged is a *non sequitur*. Even if we take the report's position, we shall still seek out moral paradigms in the realm of values and qualities. And once we do that we run the risk of saying that some people will not measure up. The separation of values and qualities from family forms does not solve the problem at all.

2. Gay and Lesbian Families

The issue of homosexuality is highly emotive; and *STC* is rightly concerned about homophobia. Consequently, what it has to say about gay and lesbian families can appear disingenuous. On one hand it seeks to identify itself with the House of Bishops' report *Issues in Human Sexuality*, yet on the other it advocates a theology and practice which by no means correspond to the general position set out by the bishops.[36]

STC's views can be summarized in three quotations:

'Many gay and lesbian partnerships and family groups…are able to create relationships of high quality, capable of expressing love, joy, peace, faithfulness, endurance, self-sacrifice and service to the outside world beyond their relationship.' (p 120).

'These families…should be given encouragement and support in the living out of their commitments to each other and to their children.' (p 120).

'We believe that gay and lesbian families ought to find a ready welcome within the whole family of God…and a fuller integration of all that they may be able to teach and give through their own particular perspective.' (pp 120-1)

The implication seems to be that gay and lesbian partnerships which are committed, loving and stable should be regarded as equivalent to heterosexual ones, even marriage. The report does not quite say that, of course, but given the direction of its arguments such a conclusion is reasonable.[37]

But the issue is considerably more complicated than this. In the first place, both the explicit comments and the underlying reasoning of the *STC* are at vari-

---

36 London: Church House Publishing, 1991.
37 The implication seems clear and follows from its assumptions about the relativity of family forms and the priority of relational values and qualities.

ance with *Issues in Human Sexuality,* despite the working party's attempt to avoid creating such an impression. In contrast to *STC's* sidestepping of substantive discussion of sexuality ('It is not our place to look in detail at the theological approaches to gay and lesbian people,' p 119), the bishops are unequivocal. Speaking of their 'fundamental principles' by which to govern pastoral practice, they argue that:

> 'homophile orientation and its expression in sexual activity do not constitute a parallel and alternative form of human sexuality as complete within the terms of the created order as the heterosexual.' (p 40).

From this they go on to recognize that pastorally there is a tension for those who, as a matter of genuine conviction, do not accept this view. Consequently,

> 'While unable…to commend the (homosexual) way of life as in itself as faithful a reflection of God's purposes in creation as the heterophile, we do not reject those who sincerely believe it is God's call to them.' (p 41).

What stands out from a reading of the bishops' document is a sense of struggle and tension between the moral theology they wish to uphold and the pastoral practice they believe to be workable. This contrasts with the discussion in *STC* where not only are the theological grounds for gay and lesbian partnerships left unstated (let alone debated) but the issue is presented as if it were merely a matter of overcoming homophobia.

Secondly, if it is not the place of a working party on family life to look at the theology which leads them to affirm the equivalence of hetero- and homosexual families, then whose place is it? *STC's* recommendations about gay and lesbian families are both radical and controversial. Yet they are offered with no theological justification other than the indirect argument concerning the relativity of family forms.[38] The recommendations cry out for a serious discussion of the relationship between sexuality and family form—yet this is not forthcoming.

Thirdly, what might such a discussion entail? The central issue is whether heterosexuality is to be regarded as morally and theologically paradigmatic or simply one of two alternatives. We see here a parallel argument with that concerning family forms. Just as the conjugal nuclear family is relativized by *STC*, so are heterosexual relationships. For if only values and relational qualities matter, the male-female bipolarity—which traditionally has been seen as a moral and theological given—can be discarded as normative in any sense other than the statistical.

The implications of this are profound. If there is no necessary connection

---

38 The (unpublished) Osborne Report of 1989 argued that since fruits of the Spirit are evident in homosexual relationships, they are theologically self-justifying. This begs the philosophical question, of course, as to whether value-free empirical observations are ever attainable.

between value and form, then sexual orientation and practice must be regarded as a mixture of biology and choice. Provided that such choices result in qualitatively virtuous relationships, it does not matter in what form they are embodied.

Against this a number of points must be made:

(a) *Man-Woman Differentiation*. A conventional reading of the creation narratives makes it clear that male-female bipolarity is not accidental but deliberate. The creation of humankind entailed the creation of man and woman as distinct beings whose individuality was symbolized by their sexual differentiation. Their unity, however, was symbolized by their coming together as one flesh. Human sexuality is therefore a matter of ontological givenness. It is not a human project, chosen and alterable by an act of human will, but a function of the divine purpose for creation. As Ray S Anderson has commented: 'there is an intrinsic distinction between male and female personhood, not merely an accidental or acquired one.'[39] This does not beg any questions about what this distinction comprises. But it does root sexual differentiation firmly in the created order.

(b) *The Image of God*. The image of God is a theologically contested concept.[40] Having acknowledged such, it is possible to construct a case which offers a reasonable interpretation in regard to human sexuality. Here Genesis 1:26 and 28 are crucial: '"Let us make man in our own image"...so God made man in his own image...male and female he created them.' Whatever this might mean, the fundamental point seems clear: it is in the differentiation between man and woman (among other things) that we see the divine image expressed.

Moreover, it is this differentiation that governs sexual relationships. The account in Genesis 1 is followed by that in Genesis 2, in which the differentiation between man and woman is expressed in the story of Eve's creation out of Adam's rib. This is made even more explicit in the following verse which speaks of male-female sexual union as 'one flesh.'

But there is a further twist to the argument. Following traditional interpretations of Genesis 1:26 as referring to the Trinity, some theologians have seen the image not merely as having been bestowed upon man and woman but as capable of expression only within male-female differentiation. On this reckoning, the bipolarity of the sexes reflects the differentiation between the members of the Godhead (the unity of the sexes suggested by the phrase 'one flesh,' on the other hand reflects divine unity). The twin notions of differentiation-within-unity and unity-within-differentiation thus link divine and human being at the level of human sexuality. Therefore human sexual bipolarity can never be regarded as a matter of human preference or biological accident. It is an ontological given, grounded in the created order.

---

39 Ray S Anderson, *On Being Human*, (Grand Rapids: Eerdmans, 1982) p 107.
40 See appendix B in Anderson above. Also D J Hall, *Imaging God*, (Grand Rapids: Eerdmans, 1986); Francis Bridger, 'Humanity' in David Atkinson & David Field, *op cit*, pp 21-7.

(c) *Complementarity and Completeness*. STC makes much of the importance of families as places where modern individualism can be countered. So it is interesting that the American theologian Ruth Barnhouse makes the same point about heterosexual complementarity. She notes that part of the rich symbolism of the creation narratives is that they attempt to safeguard both individual and corporate identity not by male-male or female-female sexual relations but only by male-female. Consequently, 'sexuality itself is a symbol of wholeness, of the reconciliation of opposites, of the loving at-one-ment between God and Creation.' Homosexual relationships must not be viewed as equivalent to heterosexual ones because

> 'Very clearly the wholeness of the sacred order is neither symbolized nor approximated by sexual practices which are thus grounded in the denial of half of the image of God. Some measure of physical or partial emotional satisfaction may be achieved, but the Christian goal of completeness is not.'[41]

Of course, it would be open to those who hold the views expressed in *STC* to disregard these arguments by saying either that they are examples of interpretations imposed upon the biblical text or that even if they may be implied within the text they are undermined by the relativity thesis.

Certainly a case could be made along these lines. But no such case is offered. Indeed, no substantive theological case to do with sexuality and family form is presented at all. And while the working party's avoidance of debate may be understandable, given the complexity of the subject, to act as if it is unnecessary is self-defeating. For without such debate, the theological basis for *STC*'s conclusions remains unarticulated. The most the reader can do is surmise from what is said. This makes genuine discussion (as opposed to assertion and counter-assertion) problematic at best and undermines the report's methodological credibility.

---

41 Ruth Tiffany Barnhouse, *Homosexuality: A Symbolic Confusion*, (New York: Seabury Press, 1979) p 174.

5

Implications

Pastoral Care

We have seen how *STC* justifies its radical views by the claim that to press (or even take) a traditional line on family issues would imperil the Church's ministry. Illiberal only in its advocacy of liberalism, the working party urges flexibility and pragmatism all round.

The problem with such a viewpoint, however, is that the model of pastoral care on which it depends is itself questionable. Nobody would deny the centrality of compassion to Christian ministry. But unless this is balanced by a clear view of truth and set within a coherent framework of moral theology, it runs the risk of becoming mere accommodation to whatever lifestyle or ideology is the current fashion. Such is the inevitable outcome of theological and moral relativism.

Collusion with contemporary social mores, therefore, is not the same as pastoral care. For such care to be adequate it must be grounded in a critical pastoral theology.[42] But despite the authors' protestations to the contrary, on every major issue *STC* arrives at an accommodationist conclusion in order not to alienate those who would disagree with traditional Christian views.[43] Consequently, while trying to be tolerant, the working party loses sight of the need to offer pastoral care which challenges as well as affirms.

Responsibility Towards Congregations

The need to care for individuals must be matched by the need to care for congregations. It is here that the working party, in its concern not to alienate those outside the Church, overlooks the impact of its arguments and recommendations upon the faithful. A whimsical example will make this clear.

Firstly, imagine a wedding preparation class. The minister is seeking to bring out the meaning of Christian marriage. She could do little better than quote *STC*'s definition that marriage is a lifelong institution embodying 'how the love of God is made manifest in the sexual companionship of a man and woman' (p 118). So far so good. The four-fifths of couples who are already cohabiting nod in assent; even more as the minister explains that cohabitation is one more 'step along the way towards that fuller and more complete commitment' (p 115) which is marriage.

The only problem is that the one-fifth of the audience who have deliberately chosen not to cohabit because they thought that was the Christian way now wonder what they were doing all along. They recognize that cohabitation is more

---

42 See Francis Bridger & David Atkinson, *Counselling in Context, op cit*, part 2.
43 A useful way of understanding *STC*'s accommodationism is to view it in terms of H Richard Niebuhr's typology in his *Christ and Culture*. On this basis, *STC* falls into the 'Christ of culture' category in which Christianity cannot adequately critique contemporary worldviews because it is too much the product of them.

than sleeping together. But if it can be regarded as a form of pre-ceremonial marriage in which love and commitment can be nurtured in preparation for the full and final commitment of marriage, then why has the Church only now discovered this? Where (they might think) is the sympathy and discernment for them in the midst of their confusion?

But suppose the minister tries to retrieve the situation by citing *STC* once more, this time to the effect that cohabitants seeking marriage should be regarded as prodigals to be welcomed back into the fold as they discover the error of their ways (p 115). At this point, the four-fifths stand up to walk out, appalled that 'the Church has been censorious and judgmental in matters of personal ethics' (p 115). It doesn't matter that she makes it clear that we are all prodigals. The four-fifths are confused as to whether their sincere cohabitation is acceptable or not. It is of little advantage to the minister that she is only trying to echo the report's 'Both-And' approach. She has succeeded in alienating everybody.

Now imagine further that word gets round the congregation that cohabitation is OK. It does not matter that they have misunderstood the subtlety of the working party's arguments. They had thought in their naivete that living together before marriage was wrong. They have, after all, been listening to preachers for years declaring cohabitation to be wrong. And if this is not confusing enough for the adults, the Church's teenagers wonder how their youth group leaders will react since they definitely do not believe in cohabitation. Even more tantalizingly, what will the minister say when she comes into the youth group to speak on sex before marriage?

Finally, what about parents within the congregation who are struggling to enable their children to live a lifestyle which is distinctively Christian? The accommodationism of the report does little to encourage them. The working party does not seem to recognize the difficulties their proposals create for sincere Christians who do not believe it right to collude with contemporary social mores.

It is in this respect that *STC* is a profoundly disappointing document, both for the Church and the nation. For it fails to grasp that there are many people—outside the Church as well as within—who long for the spiritual resources to avoid this kind of collusion. They are not asking for authoritarian morality; they simply want to be reassured that accommodation to the *zeitgeist* is not the only option and that to seek such an option is not reactionary or odd. For these people, *STC* offers nothing.

Evangelism

There is a certain irony that halfway through the Decade of Evangelism a Church report should appear which seeks to remove all element of challenge from questions of morality on the grounds that evangelism which challenges people to change will be unsuccessful. Yet this is the effect of *STC*'s arguments. The accommodationist stance we have noted is designed to minimize conflict between the Church and nonbelievers in the hope that the gospel will more readily gain a hearing.

This possesses a certain plausibility. But there runs through the report a serious misunderstanding of the nature of the *evangel*. The good news of Jesus Christ is not that God accepts us as we are but that he invites us to repent and believe even though we do not deserve to be given the chance. Then we shall enter into the Kingdom (Mark 1:14-15). The gospel of grace has a cutting edge.[44]

It is hard to see how *STC* can generate this kind of edge given its presuppositions and conclusions. If the cultural, historical and theological relativism it shows is to be taken seriously, wherein lies the intellectual foundation for challenging the humanism which dominates Western social thought-forms? Indeed, it is impossible for the report to confront them because it already accepts (perhaps without realizing) so much of the relativism which is the hallmark of contemporary humanism.

Family and Worldviews.

STC identifies material poverty as a critical element in the undermining of family life. This it sees as far more destructive than any changes in personal or social morality. But however accurate the report's social analysis may be, it is only half the story. The other half has to do with the destructive effects of contemporary Western worldviews and the moral relativism which has flowed from them. As Alan Storkey has argued in his 'minority addition' to the report (circulated subsequent to *STC's* publication), 'these cannot really be met by failure management or a relativism in relationships.' Instead, we need to see that they have grown from 'false understanding and faith commitments in our culture which need to be challenged more directly by Christian revelation.'

Storkey goes on to point out that this revelation contains the resources which will enable couples to face the pressures of contemporary culture. The gospel is not a panacea but it does present human beings in the midst of their confusion with a clear alternative—renewed life in Christ.[45] Such life entails holiness and obedience to the ways of God as revealed in Jesus Christ who is the Lord of the created order. 'Understanding the glorious creation and our place in it is the key to wisdom.' And in a telling sentence, Storkey notes that 'These themes have little space in our public and media culture; snooker has more.'

The real disappointment of *Something to Celebrate*, then, is not that it fails to understand the social context in which families live, but that it can find no way of addressing the worldviews which shape that context with any real confidence or cutting edge. Its response is so theologically weak and its sense of challenge so muted that it cannot effectively mount a counterattack without undermining the liberal principles for which it stands.

---

44 This brief comment upon proclamatory evangelism should be understood in the context of a larger and more complex theory such as that offered by William Abraham in his *The Logic of Evangelism*, (London: Hodder & Stoughton, 1989).

45 On worldviews see Lesslie Newbigin, *The Gospel in a Pluralist Society*, (London: SPCK, 1989). Also Peter Cotterell, *Mission and Meaninglessness*, (London: SPCK, 1990) especially chapters 1 and 19.